BIRD WATCH

A BOOK OF POETRY

BIRD WATCH

JANE YOLEN · illustrations by TED LEWIN

Philomel Books • New York

Text copyright © 1990 by Jane Yolen.
Illustrations copyright © 1990 by Ted Lewin.
Published by Philomel Books
a division of The Putnam & Grosset Group
200 Madison Avenue, New York, NY 10016.
Published simultaneously in Canada. All rights reserved.
"Great Blue Heron" was originally published in *Cricket* Magazine
Printed in Hong Kong by South China Printing Co. (1988) Ltd.
Book design by Golda Laurens

Library of Congress Cataloging-in-Publication Data
Yolen, Jane. Bird watch: poems/by Jane Yolen; illustrated by Ted Lewin. p. cm.
Summary: A collection of poems describing a variety of birds and their activities.
1. Birds—Juvenile poetry. 2. Children's poetry, American.
[1. Birds—Poetry. 2. American poetry.] I. Lewin, Ted, ill. II. Title.
PS3575.043B5 1990 811'.54—dc20 89-34024 CIP AC
ISBN 0-399-21612-X
First Impression

For David, age fifty plus, whose list is over 600,
and Jason, age twenty, whose list is almost 500.
—J.Y.

In memory of Ralph Steinhauer.
—T.L.

BIRD WATCHER

Across the earless
face of the moon
a stretch of Vs
honks homeward.
From the lake
laughs the last joke
of a solitary loon.
Winter silences us all.
I will miss
these conversations,
the trips at dawn
and dusk,
where I listen carefully,
then answer
only with my eyes.

WOODPECKER

His swift
ratatatatat
is
as casual as a jackhammer
on a city street,
as thorough as an oil drill
on an Oklahoma wellsite,
as fine as a needle
in a record groove,
as cleansing as a dentist's probe
in a mouthful of cavities,
as final as a park attendant's stick
on a lawn of litter.

Ratatatatatatat.
He finishes his work
on the maple tree,
then wings off again
to the pine,
leaving his punctuation
along the woody line.

STORM BRINGER

It was a dry fall
and the corn stalks
thrust through the crumpled earth
like posts
in a deserted palisade.
The farmland felt beseiged.
And then the kildeer came,
by ones, by twos.
They settled down in the furrows
and walked the rows,
brown heads nodding
over their striped bibs
like satisfied farmers
counting the harvest.
After they left,
it rained.

FIRST ROBIN

As puffed up
as a tag-team wrestler,
he hops around the arena
of our lawn.
Finding a worm,
he slips a half-nelson
on its slim wriggle.
One pull, two, three,
and the worm is up,
then down for the count,
down his winning throat.
He bobs his head
for my applause,
then looks for another worm,
another arena,
before the game is over,
before the crowds
have moved on.

CALLIGRAPHY

Duck.

                      Duck.

      Duck.

                  Duck.

Four mallards on a pond
write with the subtle
tracings of their backwash
a salutation to spring.

NESTLINGS

All babies
are born
ugly
and unfinished.
The human child
has a hole in its head
where the pulse
beats,
beats,
beats
under the fragile shield
of skin and hair.

Nestlings are
but ugly bits
of feathered clay,
too weak to
beat,
beat,
beat against the sky.
All beak and bite,
and a squawk
that links
sparrow
and nightingale.

All babies
are born
ugly
and unfinished.
But today
I found a nest with
three
baby
robins
and they were
beautiful
because they were mine.

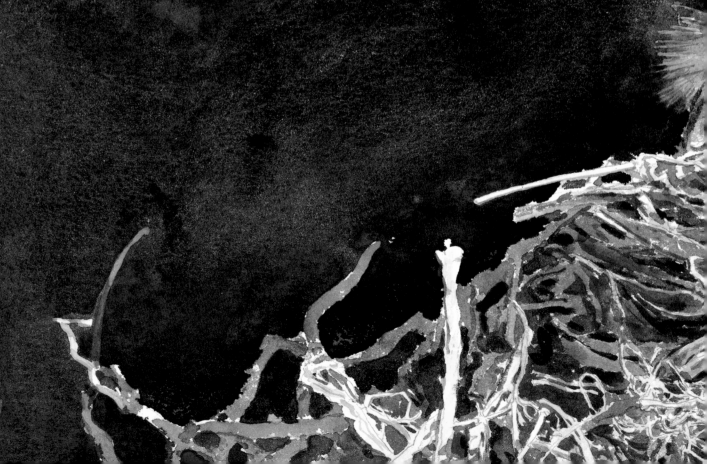

OLD TOM

Across the wet glade,
where the spring green
was still shiny and shade
gave way to shale,
the old tom strutted.
Fanning out his bordered tail
and quick-stepping, wings
sweeping the leaves,
he called his hens.

Who could see this king
featherless and gutted,
crisped and basted,
bordered with yams?
We went home instead and tasted
supermarket tom,
oozing butter and stuffing,
whose life had been short
and made for the pan.

In matters of eating,
our minds do what they can.

WINTER CHOOSING

The scruffy reds
and golds
of winter finches
puffed out against the wind
decorate our feeders.
They cling
to the branches
of the fir
and make even the bare
ligaments
of the lilac bush
flush with color
against the snow.
I choose birds
in their winter plumage
before the splendor
of our neighbor's tree
refracting
in her window;
before the rainbow
of her lights
strung along the porch.

After Christmas
our neighbor
packs away her lights,
storing strings of bulbs
in the attic.
But the winter birds sit,
fattened and glowing
from sunflower seeds
on the feeders
in our yard,
lasting long, long
past the turning of the year.

SWAN

Over the mirror
The noble swan slides
While under the surface
She bicycle rides.

Peddle and push
Go inelegant feet,
Peddle and push
To a functional beat.

Above she reflects
A pure classical style,
A marbleized stillness,
But really the while

Her diligent feet,
Her capable feet,
Her competent, practical,
Hard-working feet
Crank out one more mile.

THE CARDINAL

A showy gesture
on autumn's stage.
A brilliant blot
on winter's page.
A witty comment
on early spring
And summer's own
bright darling.

GREAT BLUE HERON

Motionless,
a painted hunter
upon a painted pond:
the brushstroked eye,
the slash of bill,
the pencil-line of legs.

Suddenly,
the head strikes,
spiking the water,
splitting it apart
with a splash
and an odd wriggle.

Easily,
the head tilts back
on the stilt of neck.
The spiked fish
slides down the throat.
One swallow—then all is still.

Motionless,
a painted hunter
upon a painted pond.

CROW CALL

I eavesdropped once
At the window ledge
And heard two crows
In a thorny hedge.

Their calls were so loud
I didn't miss a note
That came caw-caw
From each blue-black throat.

"There is food on the grass,
Plenty food on the grass."
"But a face at the glass.
Someone's face at the glass."

"There are seeds to spare,
Nuts and seeds to spare."
"But there's danger there.
Danger there. Beware."

Then they flew right off
With such raucous cries,
They shattered the blue
Of the morning skies.

Now scientists say
That a person can know
Where a bird comes from
By the sound of its crow.

Maybe one of mine
Had a Southern drawl.
Maybe one was a Yankee
With a Boston call.

But I could be wrong.
They might both have been from here.
All I had for help
Was my human ear.

KICKING UP

I don't know what bugs
My feet kick up
As I cross the meadow.
But frantic as a pup
A swallow follows
At my diligent heels
And eagerly accepts
My kicked-up meals.

TIME PIECE

Which is more fleeting:
the flicker
of swallow wings
in a field of insects,
the hover
of a hummingbird
over a flower's invitation,
or the footprints
of sandpipers
before an incoming tide?

THE DEAD BIRD

It flew up from the dried grass
into the window glass
and, surprised by the hard air,
fell back against the land.
I ran outside
and watched the beat
under its golden
featherskin
flicker once, twice, before it died.

I held it in my cupped hand
and brought it to the hearth where
I kindled a flame, hoping to reheat
its cooling life. Then
I saw it turn the geological clock
back a tick,
back to metamorphic stone:
from air to ground, buried, then gone.

WINTER FINCH

The goldfinch,
little gambler,
has spent his summer color.
He turns up
at my feeder
in his winter wings,
shabby as a beggar
on a city street.

I know that
when the luck of spring winds
returns his gambler's vest,
he will pick through
the seeds
I spread before him
as carelessly
as if they were dollar chips.

SONG/BIRDS

Along the wires,
like scattered notes
on lines of music,
sit a row of birds.

Starlings are the half notes,
finches the quarters,
and hummingbirds,
as brief as grace notes,
hover on the edges
of the tune.

BIRDS IN *BIRD WATCH*

Page 6 CANADA GEESE (*Branta canadensis*) are the Vs honking homeward. The most widespread of North American geese, they have a distinctive white patch from under the chin to the sides of the head. In migration season they are on the move day and night, stopping to graze in fields near open water.

Page 8 This is the RED-BELLIED WOODPECKER (*Melanerpes carolinus*) which, like all woodpeckers, has a strong, sharp bill used for chipping and digging into tree trunks and branches for insects.

Page 11 The KILDEER (*Charadrius vociferus*) is often found in plowed fields looking for insects. Its double breast bands look like the top of bibbed overalls. Farmers call the kildeer "storm bringer" because it arrives in storm season.

Page 12 The ROBIN (*Turdus migratorius*) is recognizable because of its brick-red breast. This bird is thought of as the first sign of spring, as it is often seen on lawns searching for insects and earthworms warmed to the surface by the spring sun.

Page 14 The MALLARD (*Anas platyrhynchos*) is a common duck. The males are unmistakable with their bright green heads and narrow white throat rings. The females are a mottled brown. These ducks prefer wooded swamps and marshes.

Page 18 The WILD TURKEY (*Meleagris gallopavo*) is similar to the familiar barnyard turkey but is slimmer. A male interested in mating fans his tail out and does a strutting walk in front of the hens.

Page 22 The MUTE SWAN (*Cygnus olor*) is a bird from the Old World. It was brought over to eastern North America and is the swan most commonly seen in parks.

Page 25 The CARDINAL (*Cardinalis cardinalis*) is a crested bird with a conical beak. The male is bright red. The female is yellow-brown but has a red beak.

Page 27 The GREAT BLUE HERON (*Ardea herodias*) is common in fresh as well as salt water. When it hunts its fish dinners, the great blue walks slowly through the shallows on long, skinny legs.

Page 28 The CROW (*Corvus brachyrhynchos*) is the black bird with the cawing voice. Flying in great flocks, crows post sentinels that call out warnings. There are scientific studies of crow calls that prove regional differences.

Page 31 The BARN SWALLOW (*Hirundo rustica*) has the large pointed wings common to all swallows. They swoop elegantly through the air, capturing their flying insect meals. As its name implies, the barn swallow is found near farms, where it nests in barns and other buildings.

Pages 32, 39 The RUBY-THROATED HUMMINGBIRD (*Archilochus colubris*) is very common in the eastern United States. Hummingbirds are the smallest of all North American birds. They have long, narrow bills which they poke deep into tubular flowers to find nectar. Their wings beat very rapidly and make the humming sound from which the bird gets its name.

Page 36 The GOLDFINCH (*Carduelis tristis*) is fond of thistles, sunflowers, and dandelions. It is bright yellow in its summer plumage and olive-yellow in winter.

Page 39 The HOUSE FINCH (*Carpodacus mexicanus*) is one of the rosy-breasted and rosy-backed finches. Abundant in the western United States, it is becoming more so in the East, where it is often found at bird feeders.